Curtiss Hawk H-75A-1

Curtiss Hawk H-75A-1. 1/72 scale plans.

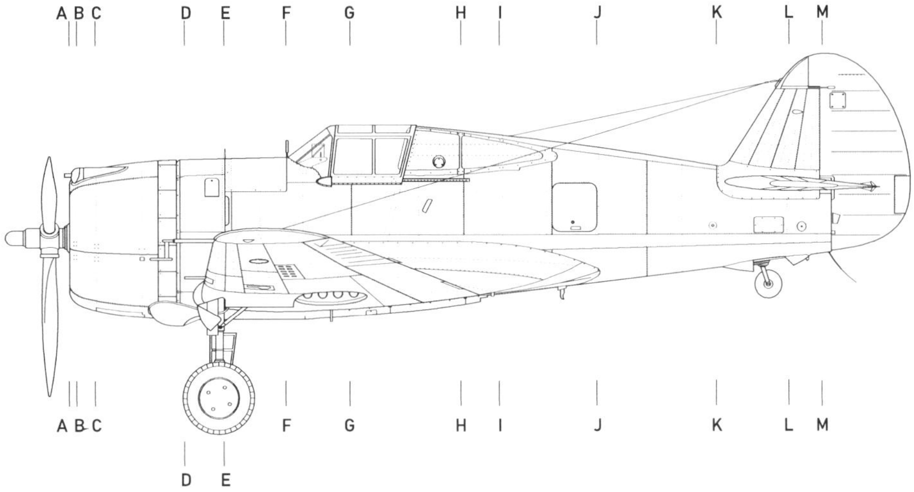

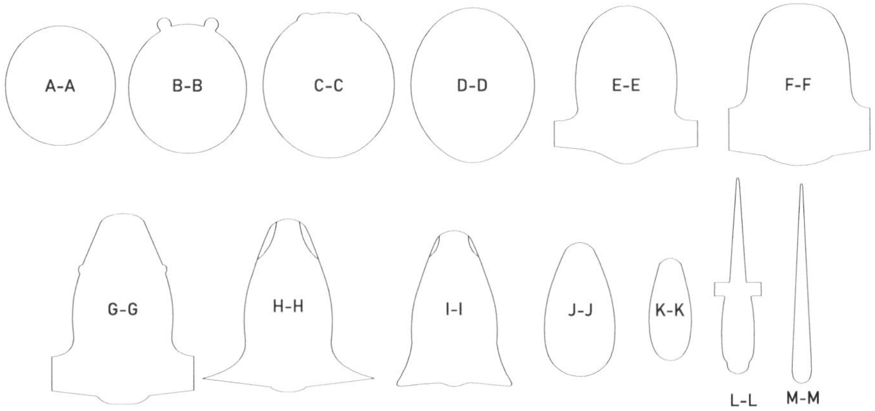

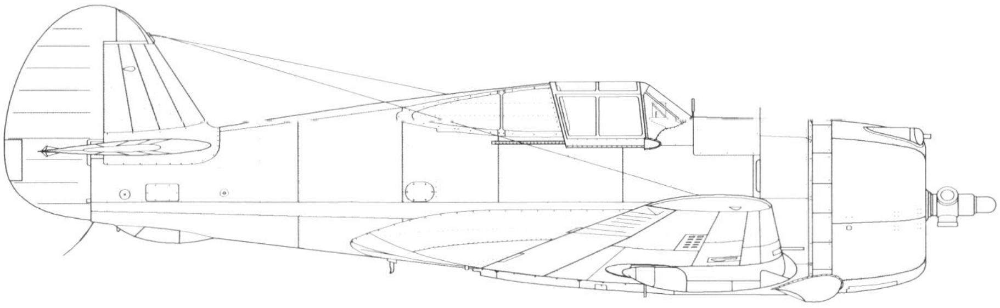

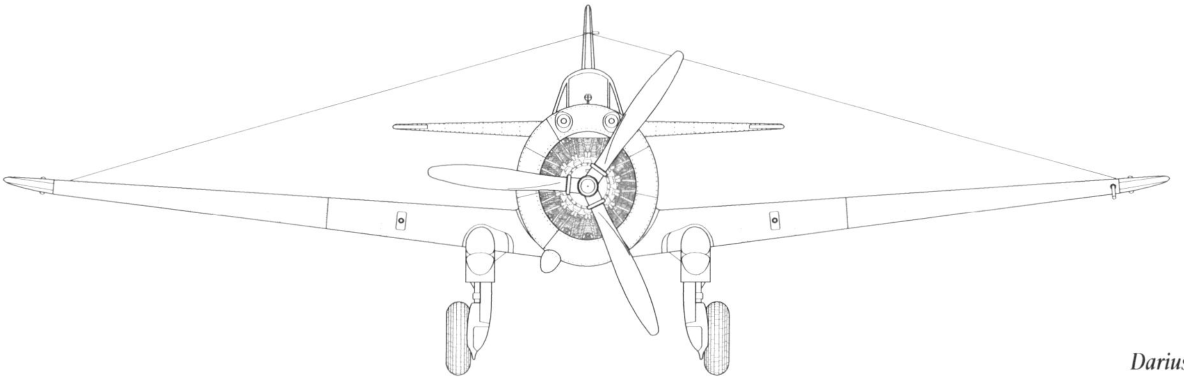

Dariusz Karnas

1

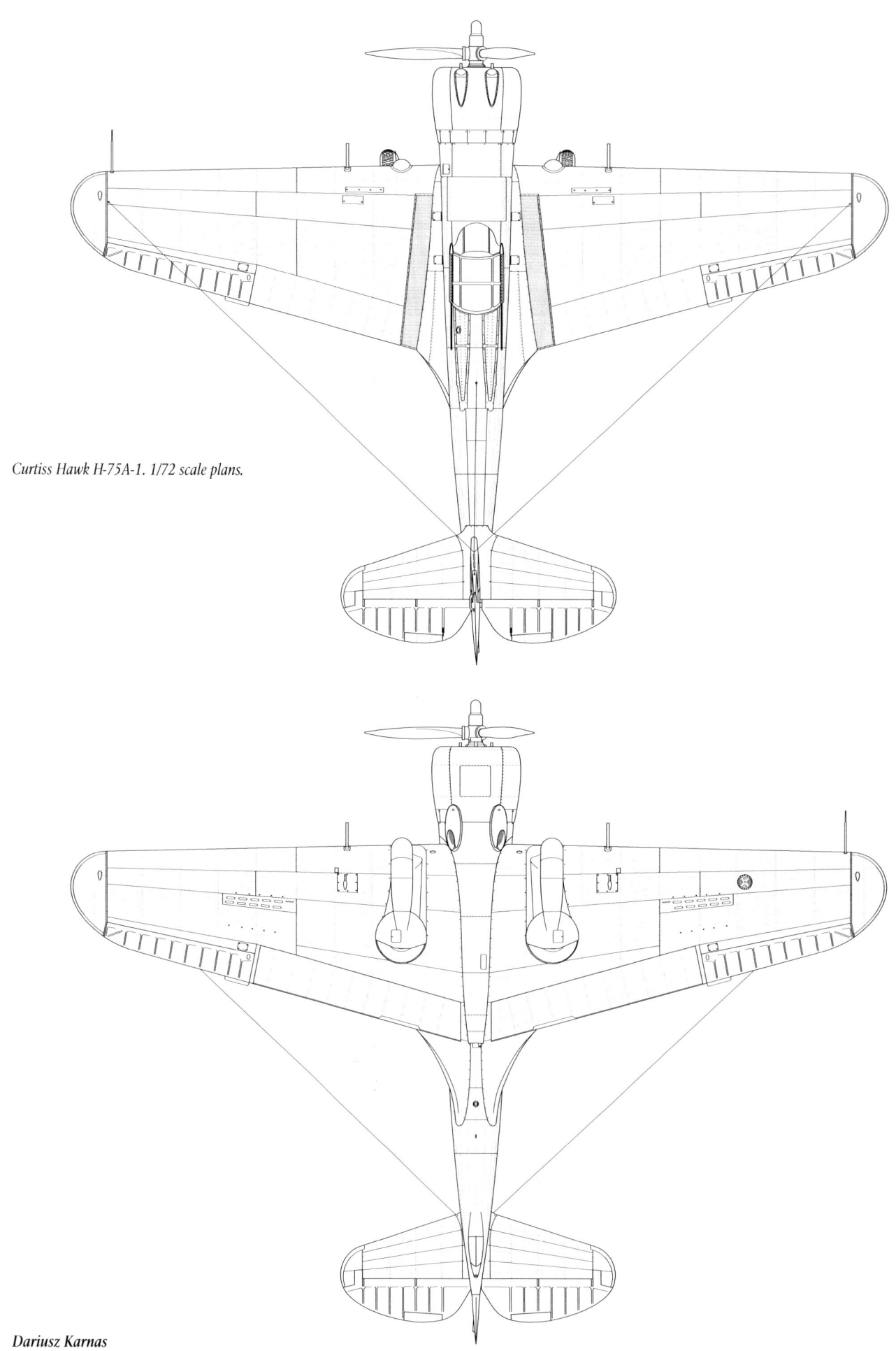

Curtiss Hawk H-75A-1. 1/72 scale plans.

Dariusz Karnas

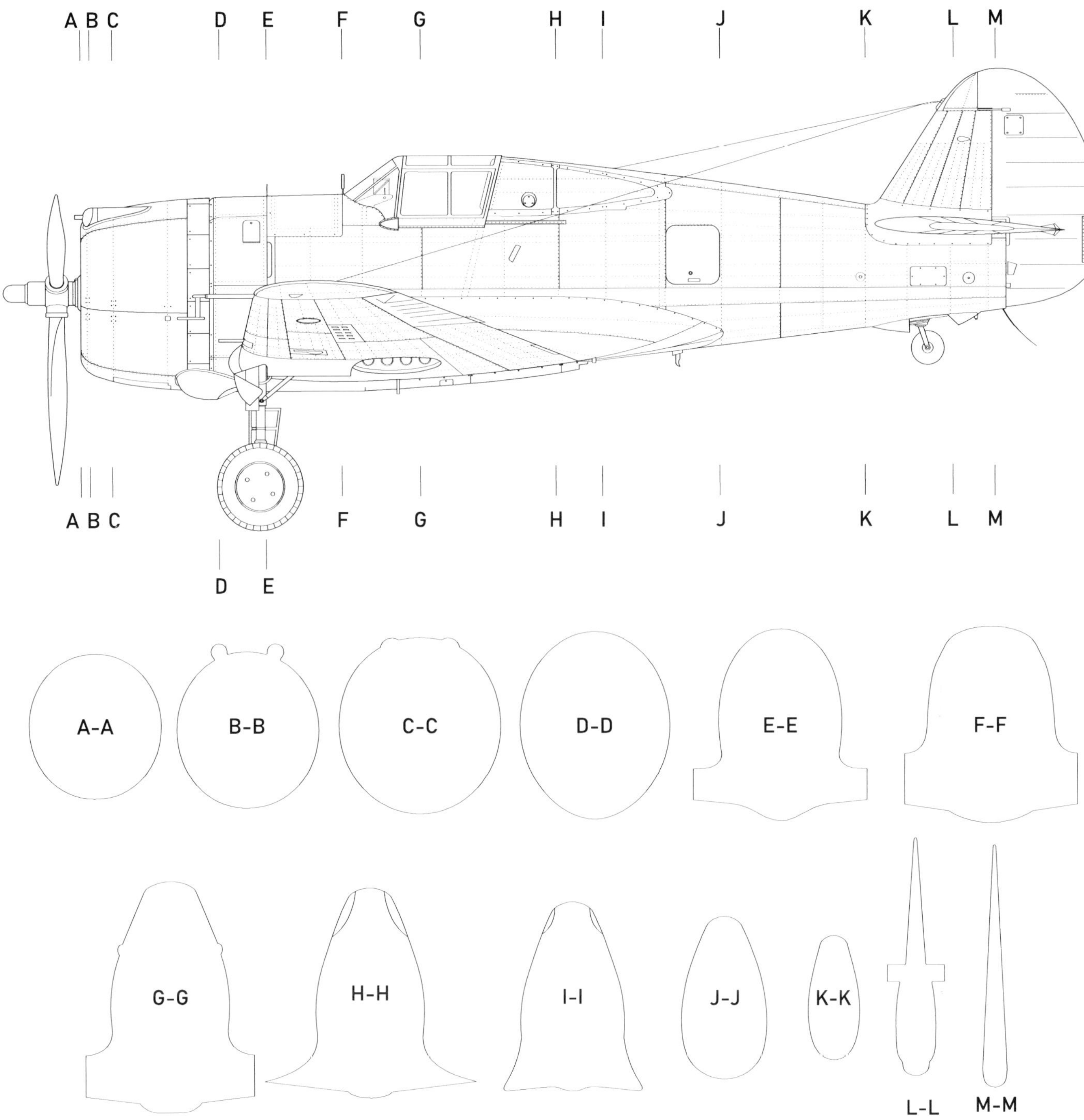

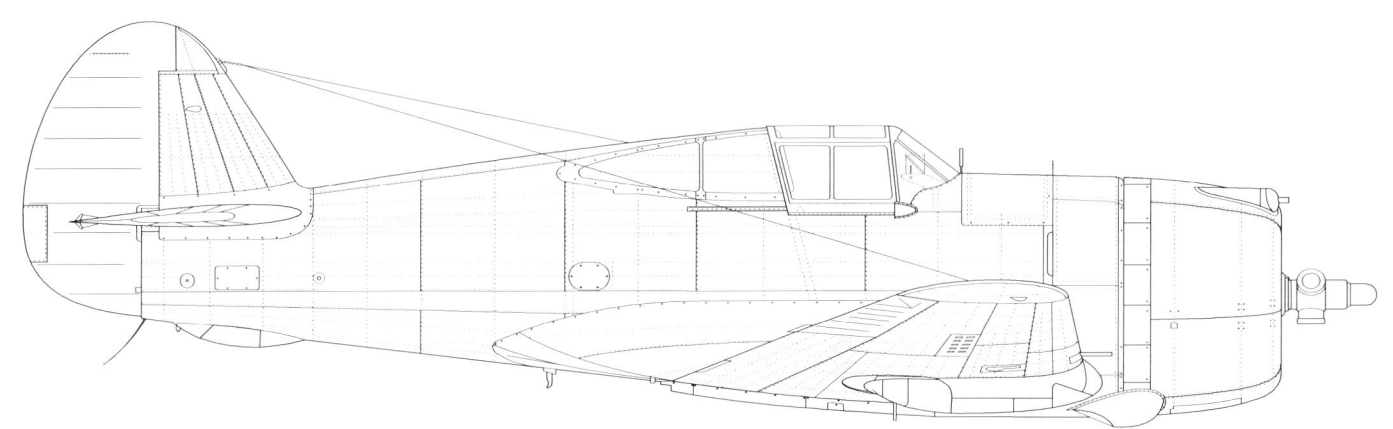

A B C D E F G H I J K L M

A B C D E F G H I J K L M

D E

A-A B-B C-C D-D E-E F-F

G-G H-H I-I J-J K-K L-L M-M

Curtiss Hawk H-75A-1. 1/48 scale plans.

Dariusz Karnas

3

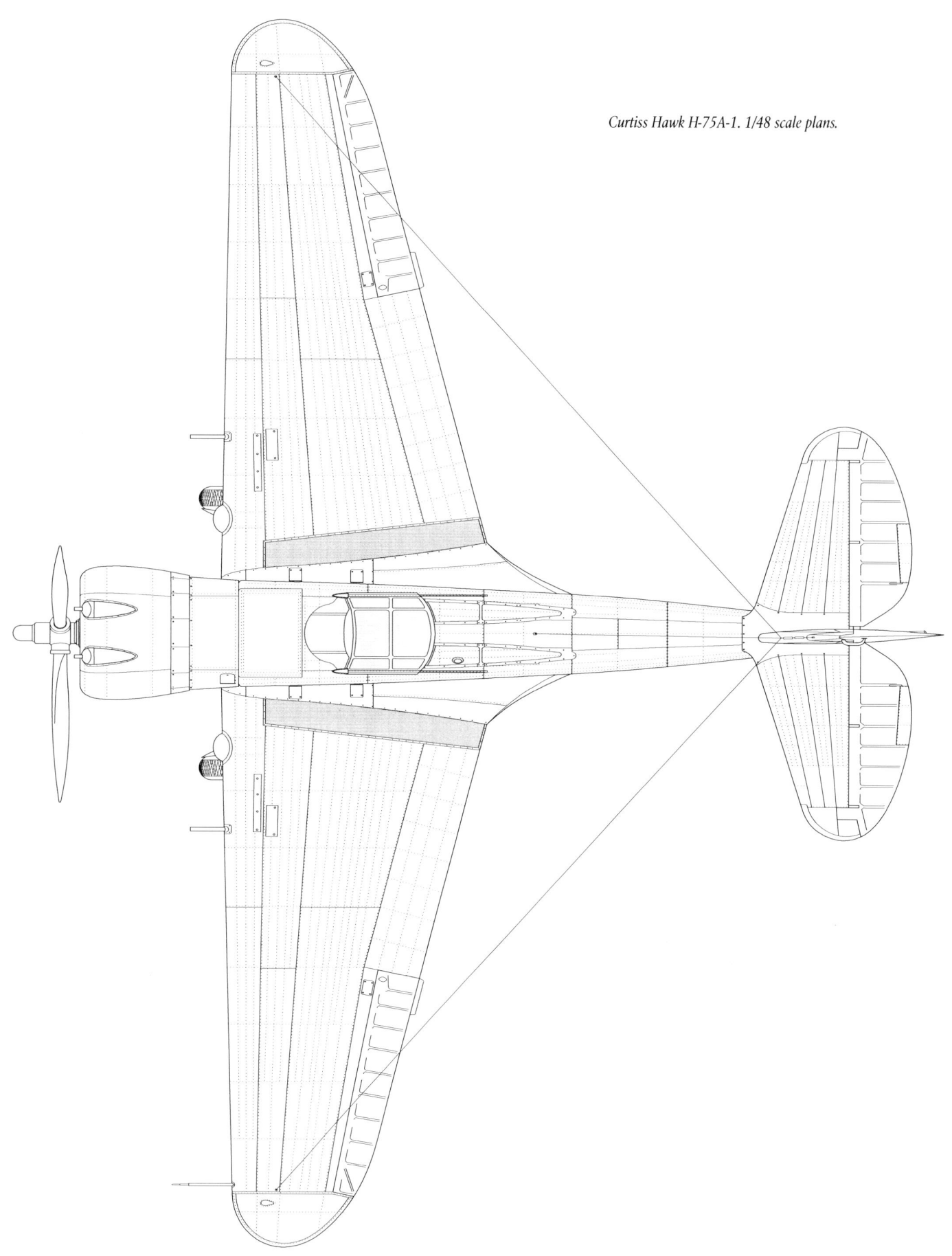

Curtiss Hawk H-75A-1. 1/48 scale plans.

Dariusz Karnas

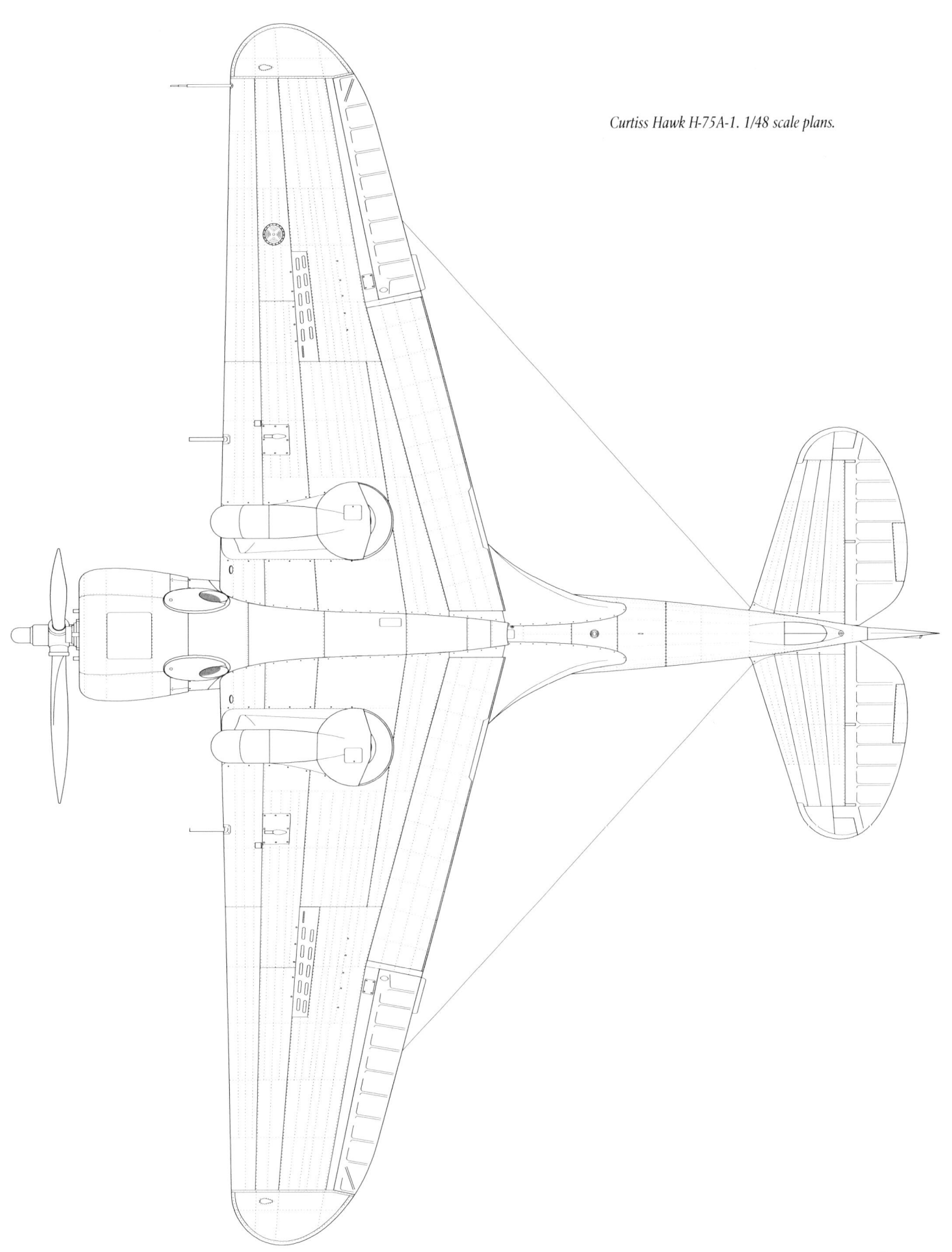

Curtiss Hawk H-75A-1. 1/48 scale plans.

Dariusz Karnas

Curtiss H-75A-1 no. 1 during a test flight in the USA. The aircraft is in natural colour of the duralumin. The inscriptions on the rudder are noteworthy, uniquely applied in black and white on this aircraft. (MAE)

H-75A-1 n°4 at the official presentation of the Curtiss H-75, when it was unveiled to the French press. (G. Botquin)

One of the first five Hawks on British soil: ex-Norwegian Curtiss Hawk H-75A-6 no. 483, which received the RAF serial number AR634. Fuselage is almost identical to H-75A-1 version.

Wings and the fuselage of Curtis H-75A-2 no. 80 (X879) white 2 of the 2 Esc. GC I/4. The underwing code is in the standardized style and position as used on aircraft with serial numbers from approximately 50 up. The position and size of the roundels on the wing under surfaces was the same for all H-75As in the period of 1938–1940.

On 14 May 1940, GC I/5 left Suippes for Saint-Dizier. Camouflage netting has been pulled over a gravel pit adjacent to the airfield to hide the Curtiss fighters. In the background is n°151, the personnal mount of Cne Jean-Mary Accart, CO of the 1st escadrille. (SHD-Air)

N°236 of the 5th escadrille of GC III/2, seen here without any unit markings at Avord. It was lost on 13 June 1940 when S/Lt André Lansoy crash-landed after an encounter with around a dozen Bf 109s. (R. Verheylewegen)

Port view of the nose of Curtiss H-75A-2 no. 107. The photo was taken after the radio equipment was replaced with German one. (K. Kössler coll. via L. Persyn)

Lt Max Vinçotte, GC II/4's 4th escadrille CO, at the controls of n°88 coded 12. While metal grids could be laid, conditions on the airfield at Xaffévillers, water-logged by autumnal rains, were difficult. (L. Persyn)

2ⁿᵈ Lt Jan Daszewski was photographed in front of a Curtiss H-75A from the Polish DAT section. (via W. Matusiak)

Ex-French H-75A-2 no. 107 as Finnish Hawk CUw-556 with the LLv 32, code no. 6. Pilot Vänr K. Tervo. Nurmoila, June 1942. RLM 71 Dunkelgrün camouflage on upper surfaces, RLM 65 Hellblau undersides. The aircraft had had its wings replaced, with two machine guns in each.

Hawk H-75A-1, CUw-568 of LLv 32 at Lappeenranta in August 1941. The fighters were parked at the edge of the airfield under the cover of the pine trees. The Curtiss fighters were not distributed to the flights, the pilots on duty flew any serviceable plane, which amounted in excess of a dozen at this point. (Kyösti Karhila)

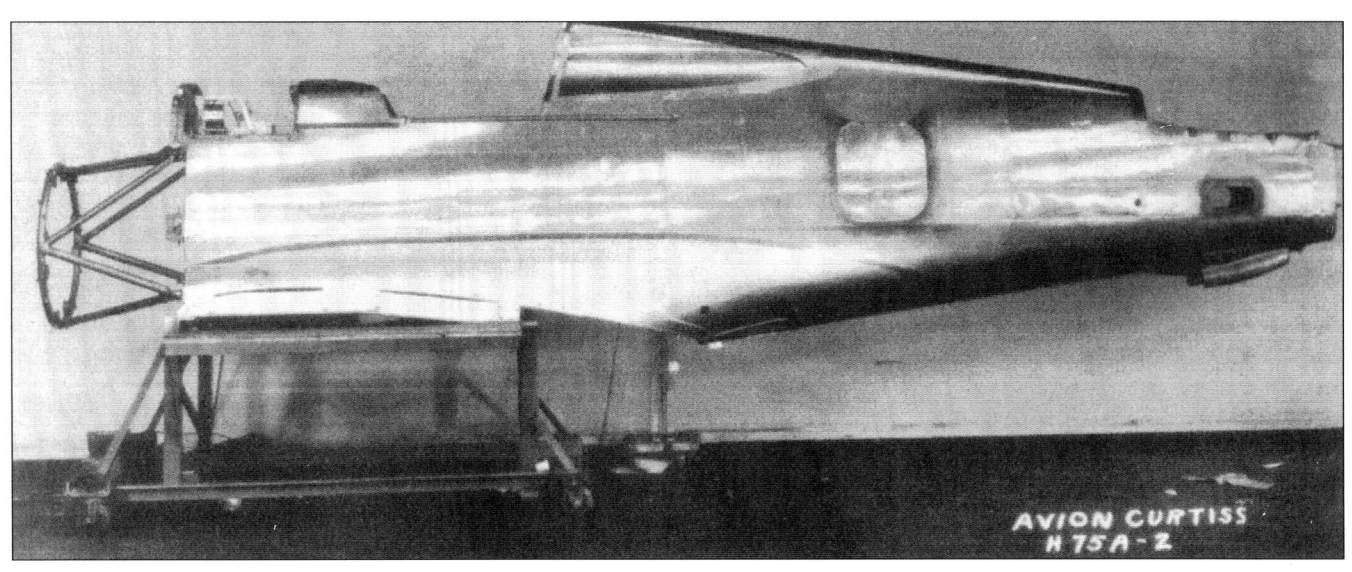

Sgt Maurice Tallent of the 2ⁿᵈ escadrille of GC I/5 in his n°18 at Suippes. (E. Preux)

Left side of the fuselage with engine mount. (Aircraft Manual)

Flap construction. (Aircraft Manual)

Main undercarriage. (Aircraft Manual)

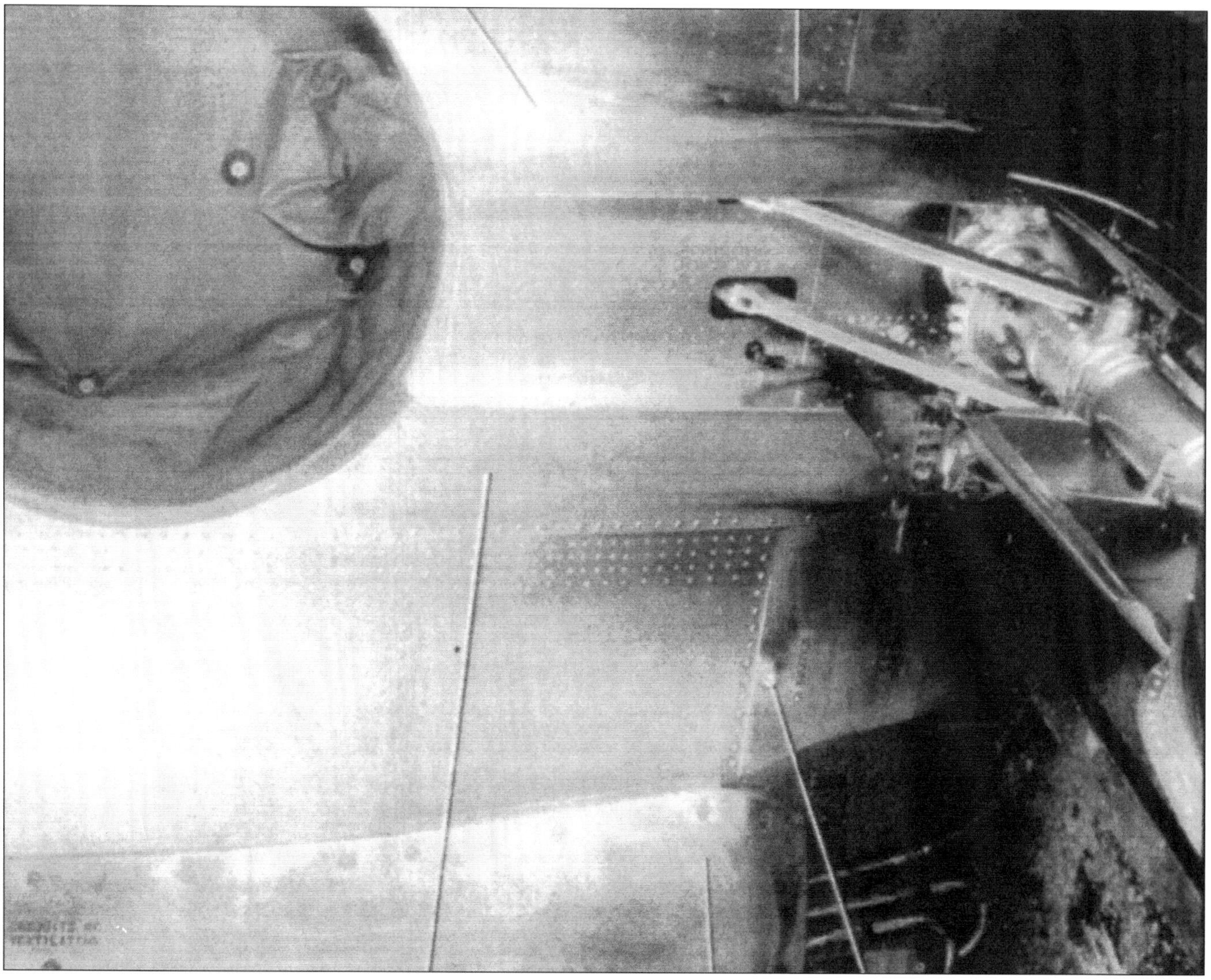

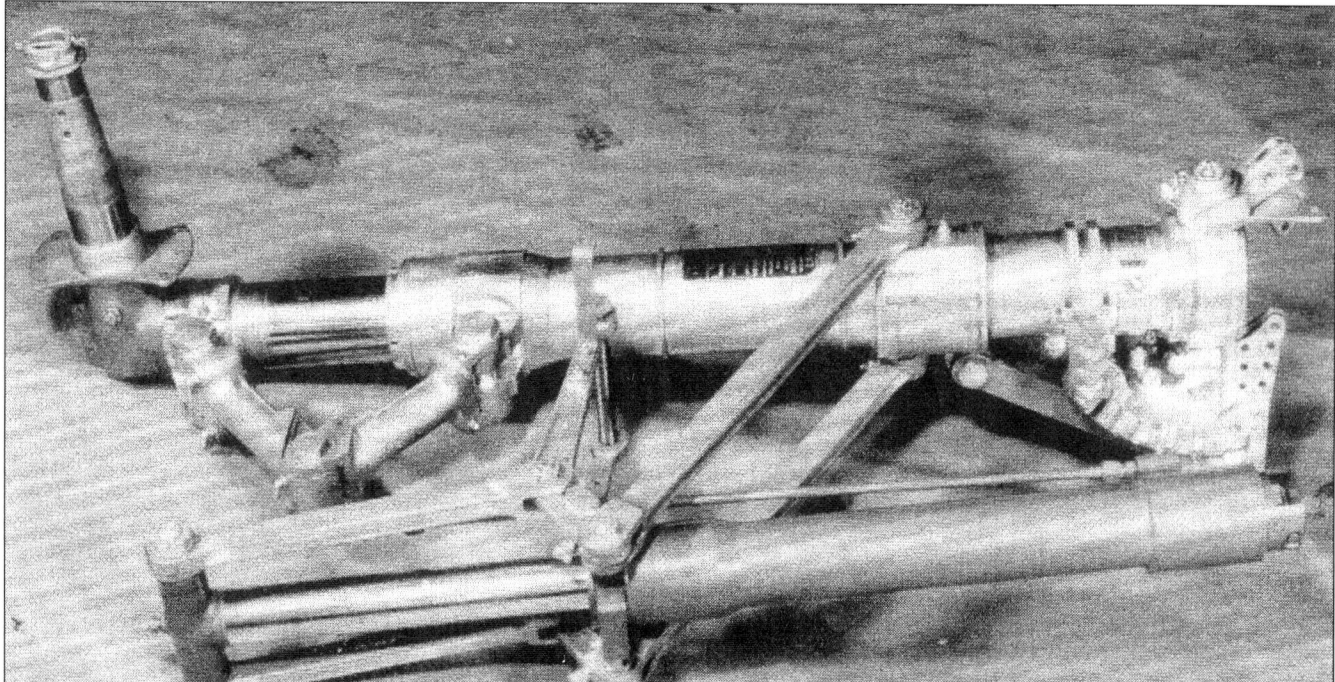

Main undercarrige leg and wheel well. (Aircraft Manual)

Details of the main undercarriage leg. (Aircraft Manual)

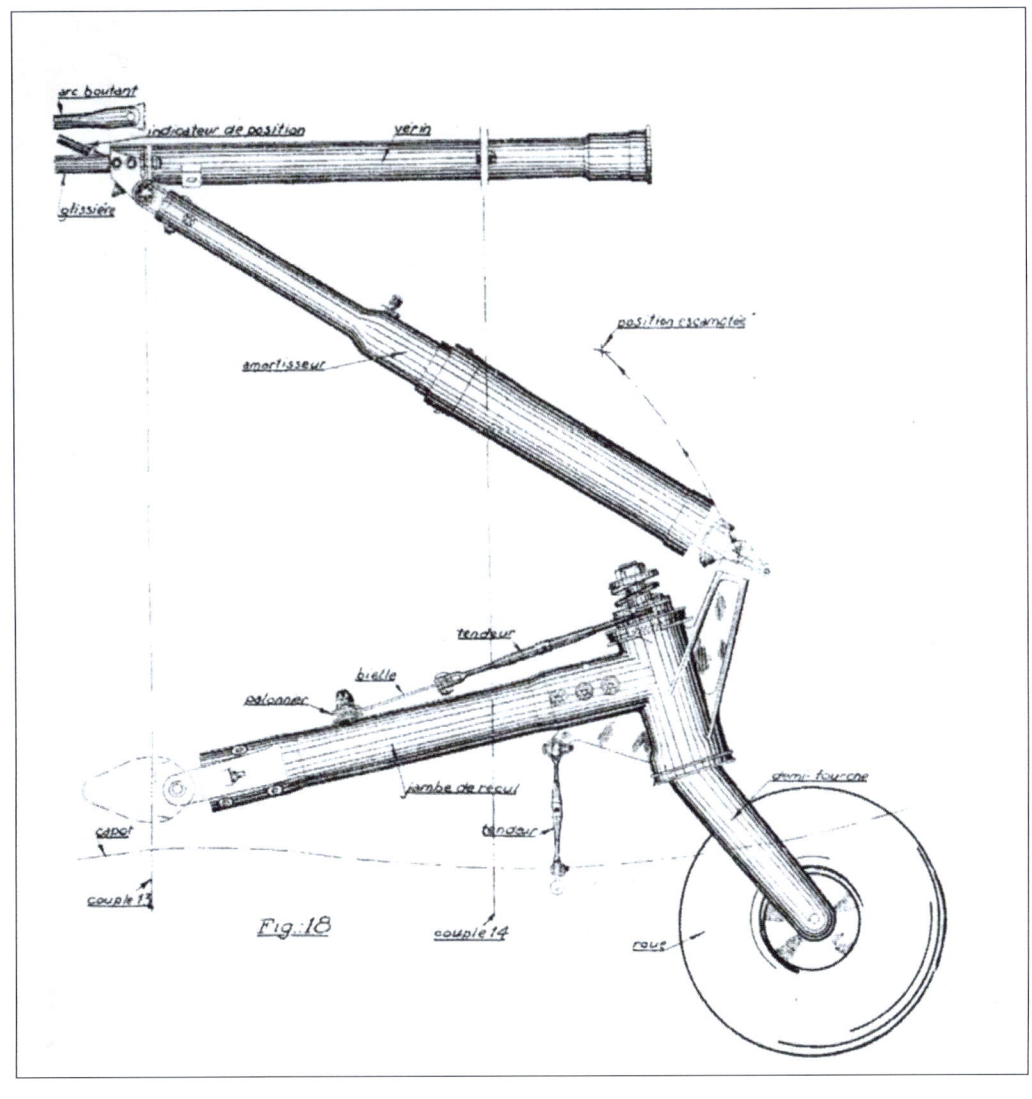

Tail wheel unit. (Aircraft Manual)

Tail wheel assembly. (Aircraft Manual)

arc boutant

indicateur de position

verin

glissière

position escamotée

amortisseur

tendeur

bielle

palonier

demi-fourche

capot

jambe de recul

tendeur

couple 13

Fig.:18

couple 14

roue

Two photos (right and left side of the Pratt & Whitney engine. (Aircraft Manual)

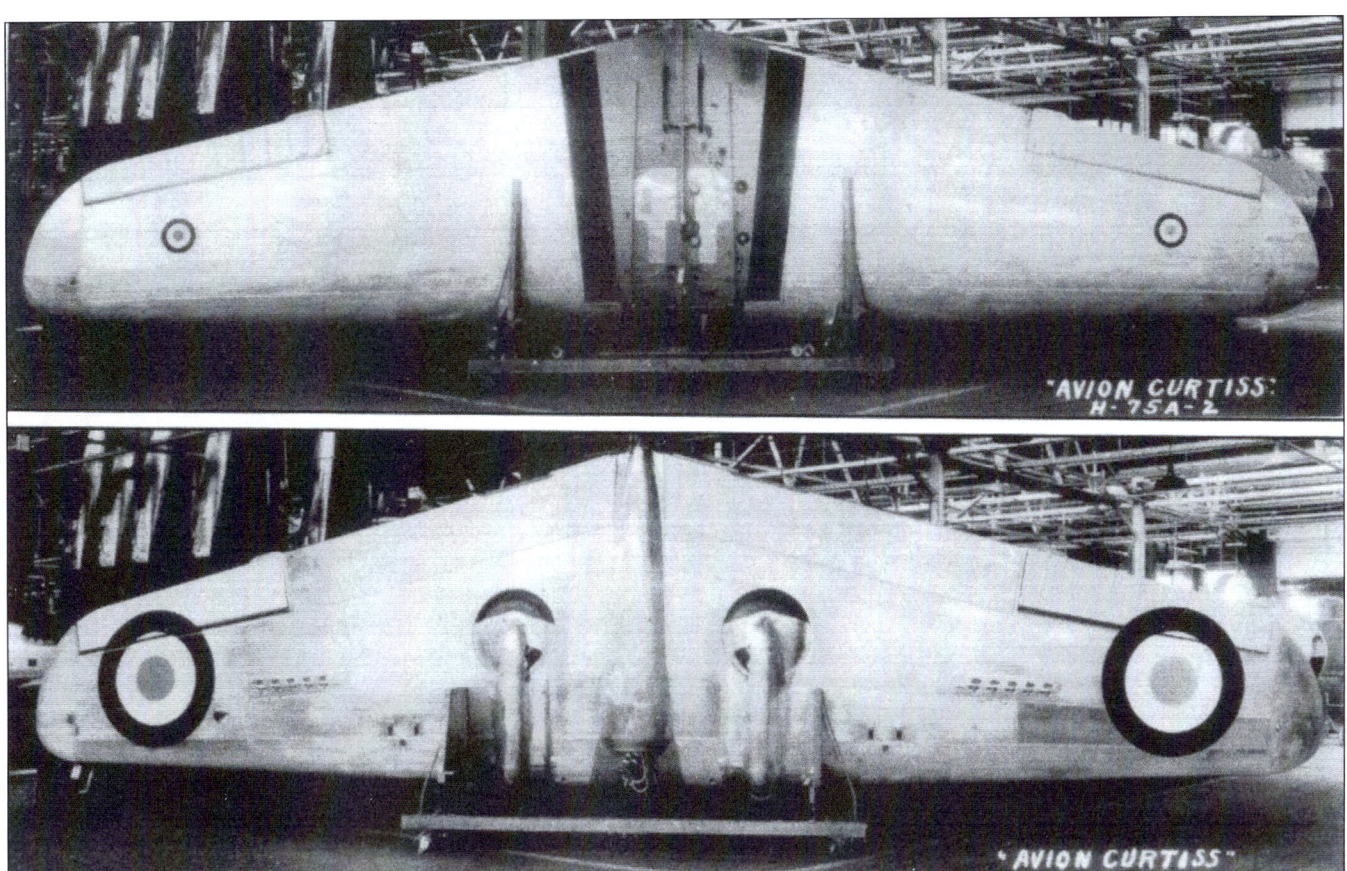

H-75 wings. (Aircraft Manual)

Left side of the Curtiss Hawk H-75A-2 cockpit.

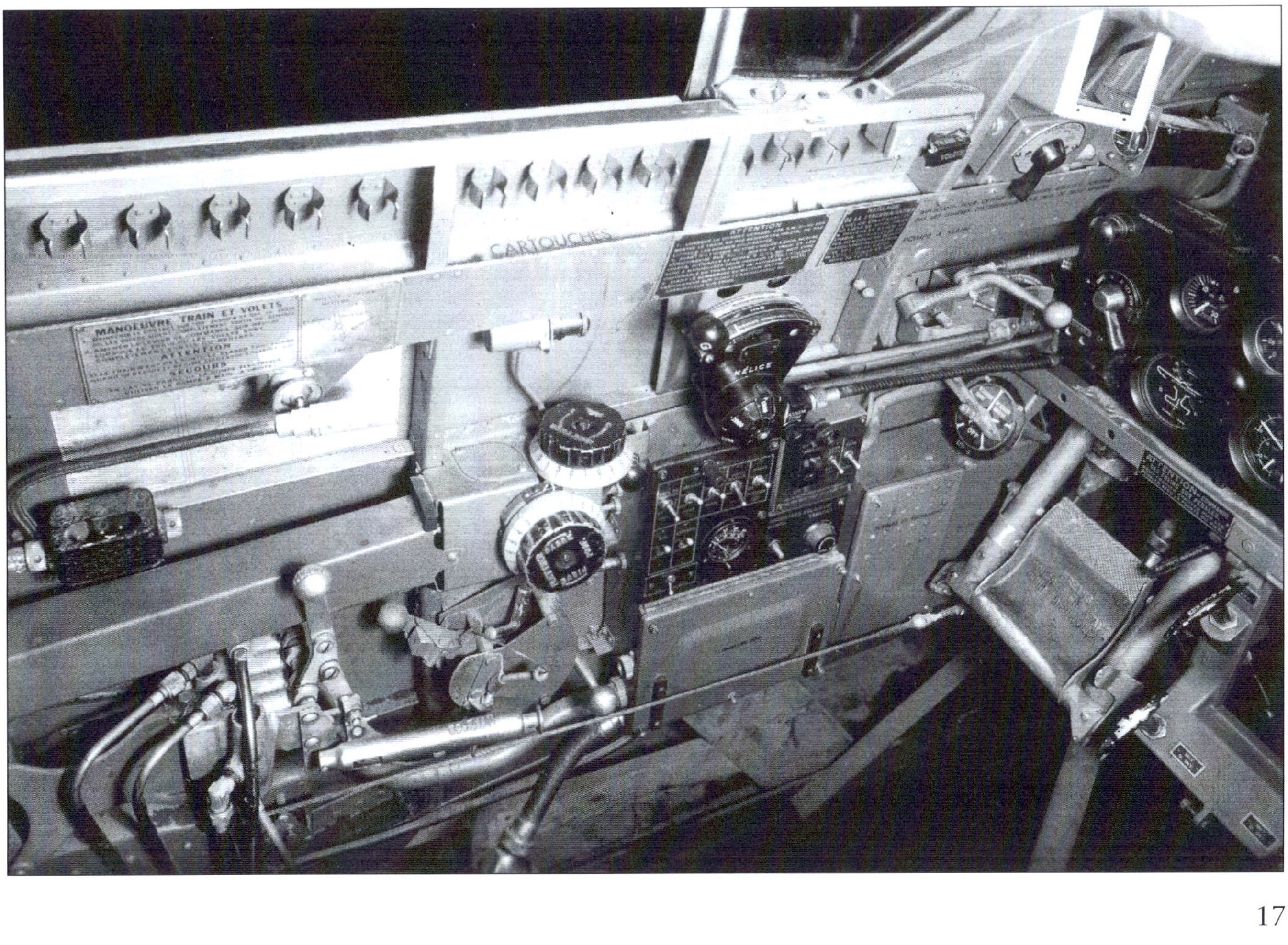

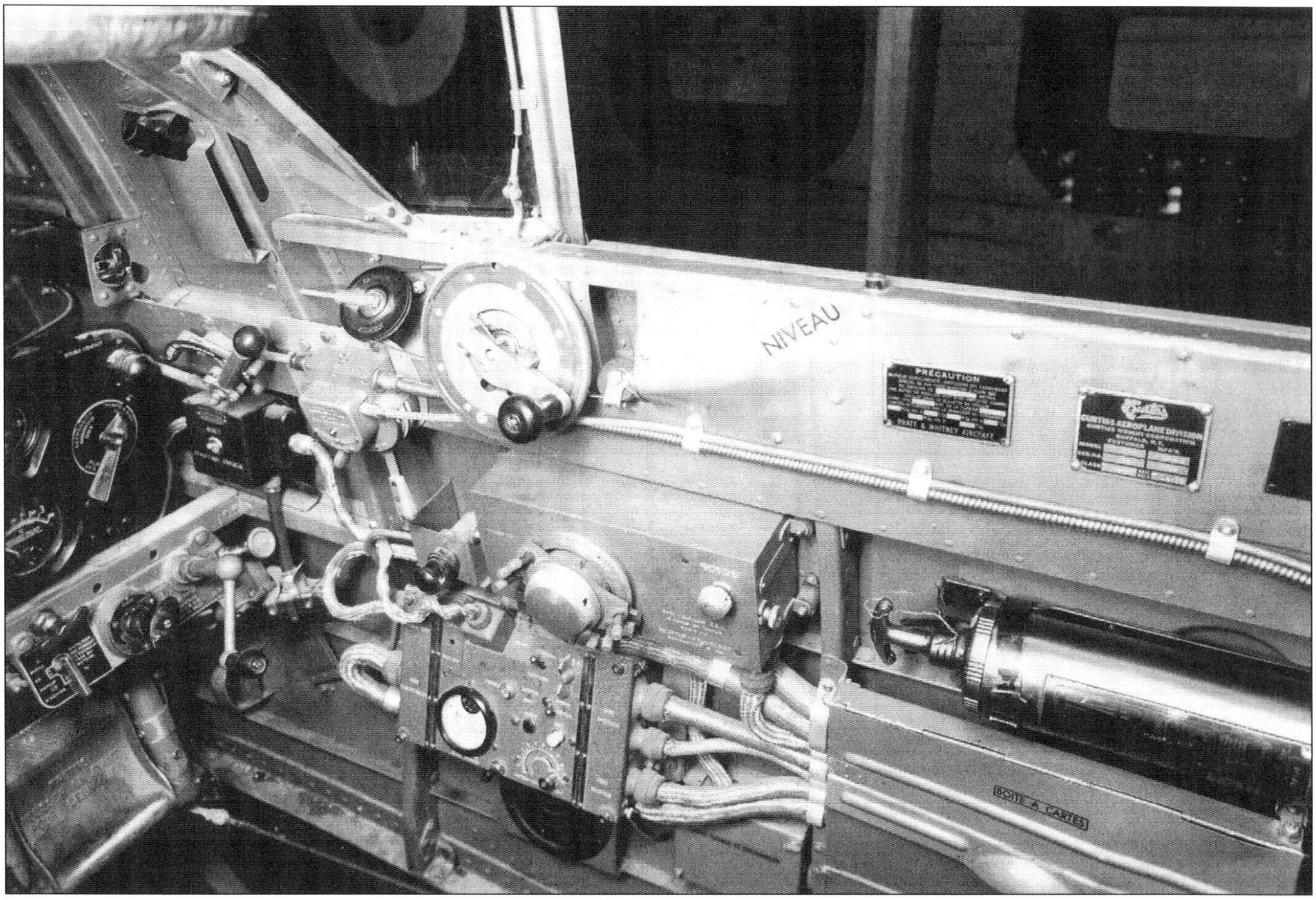

Right side of the Curtiss Hawk H-75A-2 cockpit.
Instrument panel of Curtiss Hawk H-75A-2.

Curtiss H-75A-2 no. 107 of the GC I/4 photographed in November 1939 as the assigned aircraft of Lt de Montravel. The aircraft was abandoned at the Villacoublay airfield in June 1940 and was taken over by GC I/55. Lt Jan Zumbach flew 17 sorties in it during the French campaign. Captured by the Germans in Bordeaux, it was sold to Finland, where it was given the serial no. CUw-556. (Gen. J. Tardy de Montravel via L. Persyn)

Preserved Curtiss Hawk H-75. (W. Łuczak)

Curtiss Hawk H-75 instrument panel with metric instruments.

Curtiss H-75A-1 n°26 (X825), GC I/5, 2ⁿᵈ escadrille, May 1940. Vert foncé, Brun foncé, Gris-bleu foncé – uppersurfaces with Gris-bleu clair undersurfaces.

Artur Juszczak

22

Curtiss H-75A-1 n°26 (X825), GC I/5, 2ⁿᵈ escadrille, May 1940.

Artur Juszczak

23

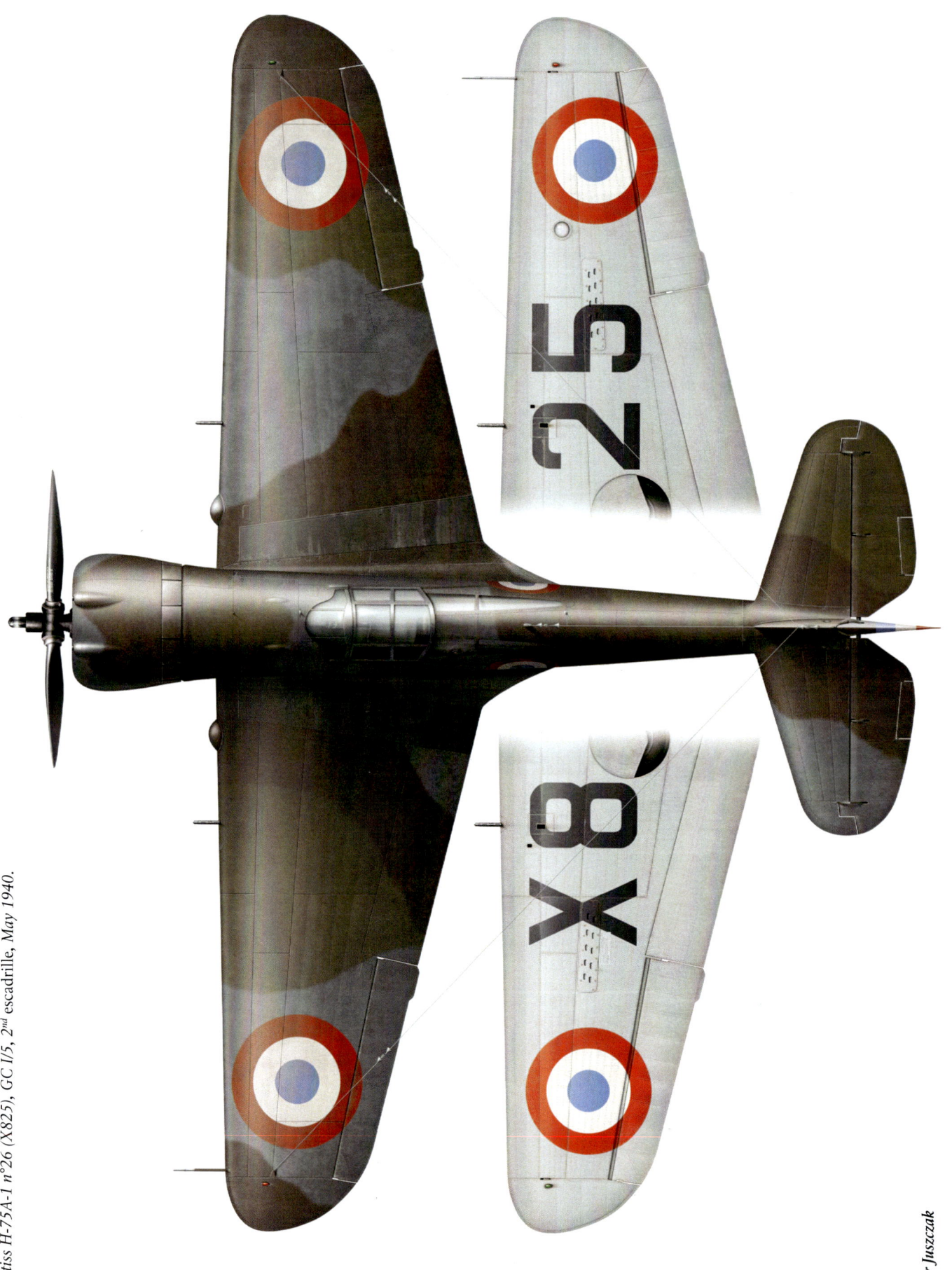

Curtiss H-75A-1 n°26 (X825), GC I/5, 2ⁿᵈ escadrille, May 1940.

Artur Juszczak